Fascinated by the two trains sitting side by side at Racine, Russ Porter duplicated the scene in a painting, but at night for a more dramatic effect. A timetable check confirmed that in winter it was possible for the two trains to meet there.

NORTH SHORE
SOUTH SHORE

Russ Porter

Heimburger House Publishing Company
7236 West Madison Street
Forest Park, Illinois 60130

ACKNOWLEDGMENTS

I wish to thank the following people for their help in making this book possible: Roy Benedict, editor of *First & Fastest* for the South Shore caboose data; Arnie Burchardt for his slides of North Shore freight motors; Don Leistikow for use of a North Shore Roster of Equipment; and Jay Christopher for the use of North Shore literature.

Printed in Hong Kong

Library of Congress Catalog Card Number: 98-75537
ISBN: 0-911581-49-9

Design and layout by Motomi Naito

NORTH SHORE

Contents

SOUTH SHORE

Introduction

NORTH SHORE

This handsome new terminal for the Chicago North Shore & Milwaukee Railway in Milwaukee was built in 1920 and was considered one of the finest electric railway terminals in the United States at the time. It contained a restaurant and soda fountain. Adjoining the terminal was the freight building which provided pickup and delivery truck service; track space for 14 merchandise dispatch cars was provided.
Collection of Russ Porter

I first became acquainted with the North Shore in the August of 1941, when I reported for duty at the Fort Sheridan, Illinois army base via the North Shore Line.

During weekend passes, I became familiar with the "Shore Line," stopping at the various towns along the way. Before that, I had seen the North Shore cars while riding the elevated cars around the Loop in Chicago.

In 1947 my wife and I moved to Milwaukee and frequently took the North Shore back to Chicago to visit old friends and shop in the downtown area.

It was much handier to arrive right in the midst of Chicago's downtown shops and restaurants than to take the steam railroads and transfer to street cars, or to walk. As our two children were growing up, we often took the Electroliners to the big city. Enroute, the kids enjoyed the famous "Electroburgers." Even today they talk about them.

As the line came closer to abandonment, the small group of railfans I was a member of went out at every chance to photograph the line and its equipment. The last day of full operation January 20, 1963, was one I will never forget. The Wisconsin Chapter of the National Railroad Historical Society chartered a North Shore car attached to a regular train for a full day of operating over the entire line: from Milwaukee to Chicago, to Mundelein and back to Milwaukee, all in below zero weather.

It was a sad day, but the worst day was one in which we visited the scrapping of the cars at Rondout, Illinois. There was a bright lining, however, in that a considerable number of the cars have been saved and are at museums around the country. The two Electroliners have been saved, with one of them being beautifully restored to original mint condition and in operation at the Illinois Railway Museum at Union, Illinois.

SOUTH SHORE

Going to and from the 1933-34 Chicago World's Fair kindled my interest in the South Shore. Living in the northwest suburb of Elmwood Park and being a steam fan of the Milwaukee Railroad, I often rode that line to downtown Chicago to photograph the steam railroads operating out of the various stations.

In order to reach the world's fair, it was more convenient to ride the Grand Avenue streetcar, which started on the edge of Elmwood Park, and ended right in the midst of the fair on Chicago's lakefront. A temporary streetcar track and bridge over the Illinois Central and South Shore tracks had been built to carry visitors to the fair.

Visiting the fair almost daily, I became aware of the orange-colored cars of the South Shore, as my streetcar passed over the tracks below the bridge. Curiosity got the best of me, so one day I boarded one of the orange cars at Roosevelt Road and went to Michigan City, Indiana. From then on I became a frequent traveler to Hammond, Michigan City and South Bend.

For reasons unknown, I took few photos of the South Shore at that time, saving my precious black and white film for favorite steam roads. Starting in the '50s through the '90s, a group of us railfans would drive to Indiana towns to photograph steam and early diesel trains. Often we would cross the South Shore tracks, and I checked the schedules usually at Hammond Station. I gradually built a collection of color slides of the South Shore via auto trips. Thus some places were omitted, while others were covered in abundance.

Riding the trains had benefits. Pictures out the front or rear windows made for interesting photos, especially on the new cars, when the windows had no nicks or scratches, as in later years.

Shops Yard was a special place for photographers. Located just outside of Michigan City, it had plenty of old equipment, and now it has the more modern cars and power to keep that interest alive.

On the following pages I have attempted to show portions of both interurban railroads in a pictorial manner and have largely left to other books the historical and financial status of both railroads.

Viewed from the highway bridge overlooking Shops Yard in December of 1973, the nicely-painted Little Joes make an impressive sight towering over other equipment in the yard.

CHICAGO NORTH SHORE & MILWAUKEE RAILWAY

In no section of the country has the interurban electric railway been brought to a higher point of development than in the Middle West. In this district the electric roads have accomplished a vast amount in developing the rural sections and providing efficient service of a character which cannot be profitably maintained by the steam roads, and in a number of instances they furnish service of the highest class between large cities, where they come into direct competition with important trunk lines.

Conspicuous among the roads of the latter class is the Chicago North Shore & Milwaukee, popularly known as the North Shore Line, whose main line extends from Chicago to Milwaukee, a distance of approximately 86 miles. This road originated in 1894 as a single-track street car line running south from the center of Waukegan, Illinois. It was subsequently extended, and in 1908 was opened from Evanston, about 14 miles north of the center of Chicago, to Milwaukee. It was then known as the Chicago and Milwaukee Electric Railroad. In 1916 the property was placed under the present management, and since then, as a result of the Company's far-sighted, aggressive methods, it has developed into one of the leading interurban electric roads in the United States. The policy of the Company has been to anticipate traffic requirements, and to provide increased facilities before they were actually needed. The public has been quick to recognize this policy, and has given the railroad liberal patronage. This is indicated by the fact that the annual operating revenue increased from $1,038,183 in 1916, to $5,677,562 for the twelve months ending August 31, 1923. The revenue passengers carried, during this latter period, totaled 15,204,758, and the merchandise hauled amounted to 355,183 tons.

The North Shore Line's right-of-way is owned outright for the entire distance between Milwaukee and Evanston, except for short distances, aggregating three miles, in a few towns. From Evanston to Chicago, the tracks of the Chicago Elevated Railroad are used. The entire line will soon be rock-ballasted and double tracked, and laid with rails weighing 100 pounds to the yard, except in city streets where 116-pound rails are used. The rolling stock consists of 145 passenger cars, 35 merchandise dispatch cars, 166 gondola and box cars and 14 electric locomotives and work cars. The Company operates a motorbus service to various pleasure resorts and points of interest adjacent to its line, and 60 gasoline units are used in this service and also for general trucking purposes. A number of trucks of the tractor-and-trailer type are used for hauling merchandise from collecting stations to loading points within the limits of Chicago. This merchandise business has increased greatly during the past few years, as indicated by the fact that the total revenue in 1917 was $105,572, while for the twelve months ending with August 31, 1923, it was $964,527.

The North Shore Line operates an hourly limited service between Chicago and Milwaukee, there being 20 trains daily in each direction. These trains leave on the even hour and the majority make the run in 2 1/2 hours, while the fastest schedule allows 2 hours 9 minutes, with nine intermediate stops. In addition to this limited service, an unusually complete express and local service is operated. The limited trains are run over the tracks of the Chicago Elevated Railroads, stopping at various stations in Chicago, and receiving and discharging passengers in the vicinity of the principal steam railroad stations. This has proved a great convenience to the traveling public.

The North Shore Line uses strictly modern equipment, and special care is taken to keep it in the best possible condition. An excellent dining car service is operated, at convenient hours, on the limited trains. In July, 1923, several parlor-observation cars were placed in service, and these have proved exceedingly popular.

A large part of the rolling stock of the North Shore Line is carried on Baldwin trucks, 278 of which have been built for the road since 1906. These trucks are of the M.C.B. equalized pedestal type, and are built largely of commercial shapes, so that repairs can easily be made when necessary. They are designed with a combination of full elliptic and helical springs which provide satisfactory riding qualities, and represent a type which has given excellent results in the most severe class of electric railway service. The trucks used in fast passenger service on the North Shore Line are designed for a maximum speed of 70 miles per hour. ***Baldwin Locomotives magazine,* April, 1924**

Previous page: Ground level photo shows the 11 a.m. Electroliner poised for its trip to Chicago in January of 1963. After the demise of the North Shore, both sets of Electroliners were sold to the Red Arrow Lines in Philadelphia. There they were rebuilt and repainted and called Liberty Liners, running out of Philadelphia until 1976. Set #803-804 went to the Rockhill Trolley Museum at Orbisonia, Pennsylvania. The other set, #801-802, went to the Illinois Railway Museum. There the train was completely rebuilt and repainted to its original appearance.

Silverliners #769 and #767 join an Electroliner in the midnight quiet of the Harrison Shops in December of 1962. Both cars were built by the Standard Steel Car Co. in 1930 and rebuilt as Silverliners in 1956.

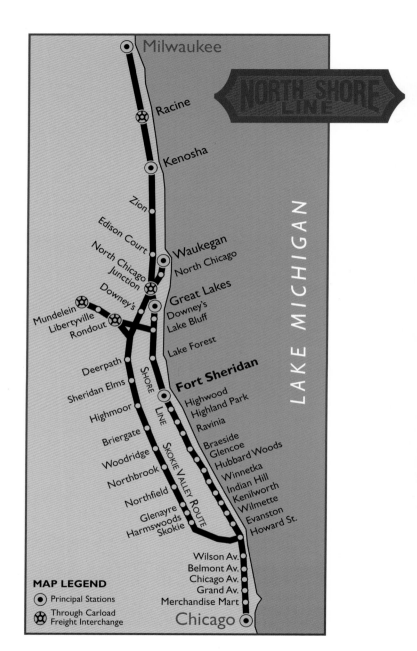

NORTH SHORE LINE

Milwaukee

Racine

Kenosha

Zion

Edison Court

Waukegan

North Chicago Junction

North Chicago

Downey's

Great Lakes

Mundelein

Downey's

Libertyville

Lake Bluff

Rondout

Lake Forest

Deerpath

Fort Sheridan

Sheridan Elms

Highwood

Highmoor

Highland Park

Ravinia

Briergate

Braeside

Glencoe

Woodridge

Hubbard Woods

Northbrook

Winnetka

Indian Hill

Northfield

Kenilworth

Glenayre

Wilmette

Harmswoods

Evanston

Skokie

Howard St.

LAKE MICHIGAN

SHORE LINE

SKOKIE VALLEY ROUTE

Wilson Av.

Belmont Av.

Chicago Av.

Grand Av.

Merchandise Mart

Chicago

MAP LEGEND
- ◉ Principal Stations
- ✳ Through Carload Freight Interchange

From the bottom of the inspection pit at the Milwaukee terminal, car #760 Silverliner looms up massive on January 1, 1963 against the light sky. Car #760 was built in 1930 by the Standard Steel Car Co. and was rebuilt in 1952 as a Silverliner.

One of the famous Electroliners awaits its 11 a.m. departure time to begin the fast run from Milwaukee to Chicago in December of 1958. The day is cold, but the passengers will enjoy the warmth of the car and the aroma of the renowned Electroburgers. None of the fast food chains today can match the flavor of that burger! Two of these streamlined trains were placed in service in 1941 between Chicago and Milwaukee. Built by the St. Louis Car Co., each train consisted of four articulated cars. The sign above the platform emphasized "38 Trains A Day." Oh, to have that many today! The workman is about to descend the stairs to pick up a bag of salt to treat some icy spots on the platform.

Above: Minutes after leaving the Milwaukee terminal in January of 1963, car #744, built by Pullman in 1928, leads a two-car train south across the 6th St. viaduct. The northbound Electroliner is almost to the final curve leading to the terminal.

At left: Two Silverliners are parked at the Milwaukee terminal in January of 1963, just days before the line stopped running for good. A number of these cars were rebuilt in the 50s to complement the famed Electroliners. The cars were shiny red above the belt rail; below the body was painted to imitate fluted stainless steel. The interiors were also modernized with new seat fabrics, blue and gray floors, large photo murals and stainless steel fittings.

On January 19, 1963 Silverliner #409 and coach #741, along with others, wait on the Milwaukee terminal storage tracks for a call which will never come. Two days later, the North Shore ceased to exist. Car #409 was built by the Cincinnati Car Company in 1923 as a diner, rebuilt in 1942 as a coach and then rebuilt in 1955 as a Silverliner. Coach #741 was built by Pullman in 1928.

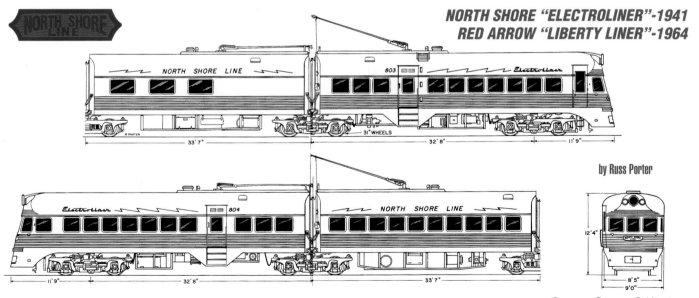

Above left: Light snow has stopped, and the platform attendant has already scattered salt from the bag on the cart. The North Shore cannot afford liability lawsuits for injuries in its final days. The Electroliner is being serviced for a trip to Chicago, while the Silverliner across the platform has recently come in from Chicago. Date: January 19, 1963.

Above right: An Electroliner has just arrived in Milwaukee in February of 1960 and the *Chicago Limited* is ready to receive passengers. Its name is no mere bragging, as it regularly ran between the two cities at 70-80 mph.

NORTH SHORE "ELECTROLINER"-1941
RED ARROW "LIBERTY LINER"-1964

by Russ Porter

Courtesy Carstens Publications

Above: Just minutes away from its Milwaukee terminal destination, an Electroliner from Chicago slows down on the 6th St. viaduct on January 19, 1963.

At right: With automobile traffic halted, the 11 a.m. Electroliner for Chicago twists around the sharp curves leading out of the Milwaukee terminal in December of 1958.

At left: Although years and miles of travel show, this grimy veteran still makes a dramatic sight, towering over the inspection pit at the Milwaukee terminal in 1962.

Above: Slowly pulling away from the Milwaukee terminal and around the sharp curve on the hill, the 2 p.m. Electroliner heads toward the 6th St. viaduct and Chicago in January of 1963.

Above: In November of 1962 combine #250, re-splendent in new paint, has recently arrived at the Milwaukee terminal. Everything from frozen fish to newspapers was carried in the small baggage area of #250. Seven of these combines were built by the Jewitt Car Co. in 1917. Car #251 was made into a Silverliner in 1953 and eventually went to the Illinois Railway Museum.

At left: In November of 1962 a workman inspects one of the cars in the storage yard at the Milwaukee terminal. Small repairs were made here, with larger ones at Harrison or Highwood shops. By their dingy appearance it would seem that a wash job is due, and that was performed at Highwood.

Two Silverliners are part of a Chicago-bound train coming upgrade on the 6th St. viaduct in Milwaukee in May of 1961. A repair session on the viaduct is in progress, providing the motorman with another headache.

Wood parlor-buffet car #401 was one of three cars put into dining car service in 1910. Similar steel cars were obtained in 1917 by the North Shore. Shortly after, the three wood cars 400-402 were converted for use as coaches. This change required removal of the kitchen and installation of walkover seats. In 1936, #400 was retired, and the 401-402 went to the Chicago, Aurora & Elgin Railroad. *Collection of Russ Porter*

The Electroliner has been serviced and is ready to receive Chicago-bound passengers for an 8 p.m. departure time at the Milwaukee terminal. The old coach at the left seems subdued in the bright glowing colors of the Electroliner. Date: January, 1962.

The North Shore had a thriving business in small package goods delivered via seven fast combine-equipped trains. Here we see an employee unloading frozen fish onto a waiting cart at the Milwaukee terminal in January of 1962.

With its red marker and small emergency lights on, an Electroliner from Chicago is being serviced at the Milwaukee terminal in January of 1962. Soon a trainman will turn out the two lights and passengers will be allowed on the platform to fill the train for its 8 p.m. departure.

Even from ground level at Milwaukee, an Electroliner and standard coach make a beautiful night-time scene, especially on a very cold evening in November of 1962.

Above: A two-car train has just picked up passengers at Harrison St. on the south side of Milwaukee in April of 1959 and will soon enter the private right-of-way to Chicago.

At left: Ironically, the front doorway and the glass sign above the doors were the last remaining parts of the Milwaukee terminal still standing after its razing in 1964. Through these doors passed thousands of passengers between 1920 and January 20, 1963.

Unfortunately, the North Shore never obtained a private right-of-way to its terminal in Milwaukee. Slow running on the city streets was a problem, especially during winter months. Here on January 12, 1963 a northbound Electroliner wheels cautiously down 5th St. toward the terminal.

What a contrast! A gleaming Chicago-bound Electroliner stops for a few minutes at Harrison St. next to car #232, now in rundown condition. It started life as a merchandise express car built in 1924 by the Cincinnati Car Co. When business declined, #232 was converted to work service in 1947. The car was scrapped at Rondout, Illinois.

With automobile headlights shining on its side, an Electroliner provides a spectacular night scene at the Harrison St. stop on January 16, 1963.

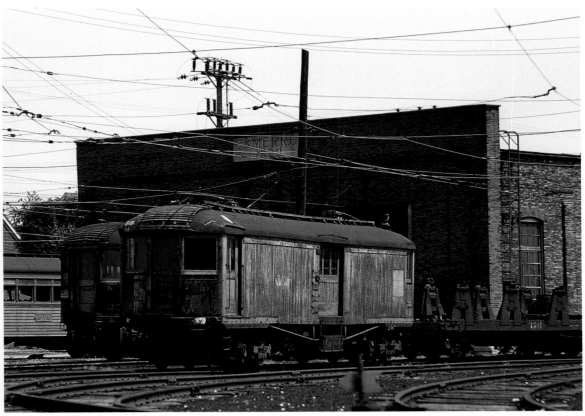

Above: Three styles of equipment stand on trackage at the Harrison Shops in Milwaukee on August 7, 1961: a Silverliner on the left, a standard coach in the middle and work car #232 on the right. The sign above the shop building still reads "C&M RR Co. 1890," which translated meant "Chicago & Milwaukee R.R. Co.," a sign that lasted until the building was torn down, even though the railroad was reorganized as the Chicago North Shore & Milwaukee Railway in 1916.

At left: Even near the end of North Shore operations, passenger cars were kept in good mechanical condition. Harrison Shops in Milwaukee was an important maintenance point for the north end of the railroad.

Sailors from the Great Lakes Training Station alight from a northbound Silverliner at 5th and Harrison St. in Milwaukee. Snow and a biting cold wind makes it miserable to walk any distance on this January afternoon in 1963.

A youngster has a choice viewing seat in the front of a southbound Electroliner as it makes a short stop at Harrison St. in October of 1962. From Harrison St. the train will proceed on its own high-speed right-of-way.

Beginning in 1926, the North Shore was the first railroad in the United States to offer truck-trailer piggyback service. Freight motor #450 picks up some trailer loads at Harrison Shops in the 1940s. After World War II, super highways and the growth of truck competition caused the North Shore to eliminate this operation in 1947. This steeple locomotive was built by General Electric in 1907.
Collection of Arnie Burchardt

Plow #238, sitting on a service track at Harrison Shops in June of 1961, was originally built as a merchandise dispatch car in 1924 by the Cincinnati Car Co. In 1949 it was converted to a plow and scrapped in February of 1964 at Rondout.

Coach #748 and combine #256 line up at the entrance to Harrison Shops in 1962. Coach #748 was built in 1928 by Pullman. Combine #256 was built in 1917 by Jewitt Car Co. Both cars were scrapped at Rondout.

Combine #252 is at Harrison Shops in December of 1962. Built by the Jewitt Car Co. in 1917, it was scrapped at Rondout, Illinois in December of 1963.

A January, 1963 snowstorm is blowing off Lake Michigan as a northbound train passes the Harrison St. shelter at Milwaukee. The train, nicknamed "Sailors Special" because of the large group of sailors aboard on a weekend pass, will be at the Milwaukee terminal within minutes.

Above: Sporting a brand-new paint job, Silverliner #738 gleams in the morning sun in February of 1960 at Harrison Shops, Milwaukee. Built in 1918 by Pullman as a coach, it was rebuilt as a Siverliner in 1950.

At left: It is 5:10 a.m. on January 20, 1963, and the temperature outside is minus 5 degrees, as a last photo of an Electroliner is taken at Harrison Shops, Milwaukee. The North Shore ceased operating at 4:01 a.m. on January 21, 1963.

Still attractive in something of a traction orange, tool car #235 is on a storage track next to Harrison Shops in April of 1955. Car #235 was built in 1924 by the Cincinnati Car Co. as a merchandise dispatch car and was rebuilt for use in sleet train service. It was burned at Highwood in June of 1959.

Two Silverliners have some interior work done at Harrison Shops in November of 1962. A closeup of the sides under the windows shows the clever painting to simulate fluted stainless steel.

A train stop of just a few minutes allowed a tripod-mounted camera to record this night scene at Harrison St. on January 11, 1963.

Above: It's 5 a.m. January 20, 1963, and an Electroliner sits quietly inside the warm Harrison Shops. Outside the temperature is minus five degrees. This will be the last day of full operation for this train.

At left: Christmas decorations are still to be seen as a North Shore car leaves Harrison St. northbound on 5th St. on its way to its Milwaukee terminal in January of 1963.

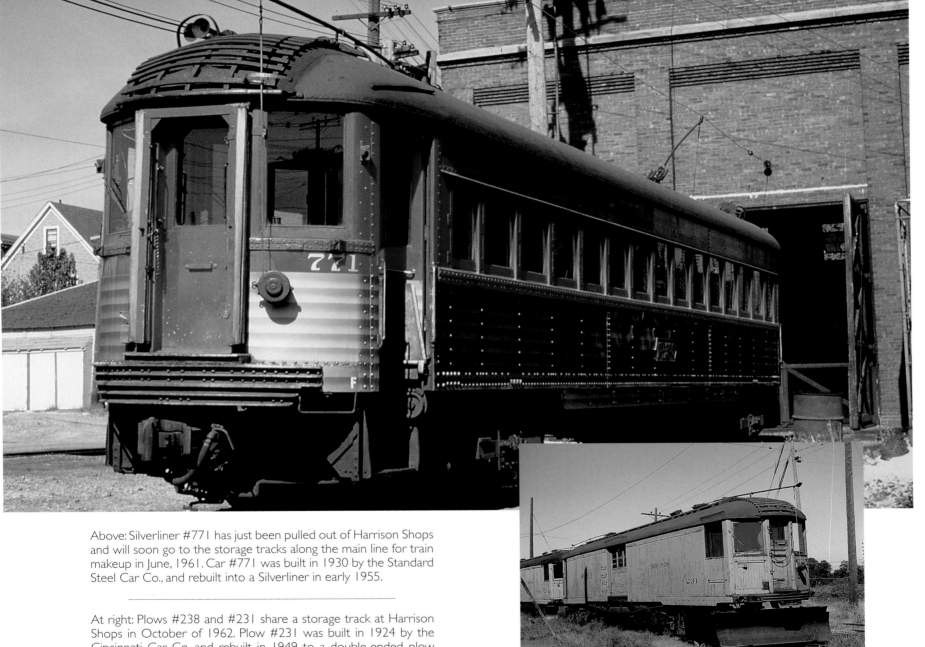

Above: Silverliner #771 has just been pulled out of Harrison Shops and will soon go to the storage tracks along the main line for train makeup in June, 1961. Car #771 was built in 1930 by the Standard Steel Car Co., and rebuilt into a Silverliner in early 1955.

At right: Plows #238 and #231 share a storage track at Harrison Shops in October of 1962. Plow #231 was built in 1924 by the Cincinnati Car Co. and rebuilt in 1949 to a double-ended plow with air-operated wings.

Above: On a beautiful warm August day in 1962, a four-car south-bound Silverliner picks up speed on the girder bridge over the Chicago & NorthWestern tracks, tracks that join Milwaukee with the capital city of Madison. Just a few minutes before, the train had passed Harrison Shops.

At left: The side of combine #253 shines brightly in the glow of an automobile's headlights at Harrison Shops in January, 1963. The combine was built in 1917 by the Jewitt Car Co.

Above: With a blast of its air horn, northbound combine, with two Silverliners trailing, hurls toward the College Ave. bridge in June 1961.

At right: A Chicago-bound Electroliner crosses over Oklahoma Ave. on the south side of Milwaukee in August of 1962.

Traveling nearly 70 miles an hour, southbound Electroliner is about to go under the College Ave. bridge in June of 1961.

Above: Horn blowing, a 70 mph Chicago-bound Electroliner in December of 1961 is about to cross a country road just south of Ryan Tower, whose signal lights are just visible between poles and the last car.

At right: A three-car northbound train crosses the massive girder bridge over the Root River near Racine in 1962.

A southbound Silverliner, with horns blowing, crosses Highway 31 near Racine on a sunny but cold day in January of 1963.

Merchandise dispatch car #6, shown at Racine around 1910, was built by the Brill Co. in 1902.
It lasted until 1930 and was stored until 1936 when it was scrapped. *Collection of Russ Porter*

Northbound Electroliner gathers speed leaving Racine in June of 1953. The southbound platform is filling up with passengers awaiting a train due any minute.

Many of the North Shore freight motors made Pettibone Yard their home terminal.
Here in July, 1962 is motor #458, left; motor #455, center; and motor #453, right.
Collection of Arnie Burchardt

At right: Line car #604 is shown in June of 1962 at Pettibone Yard, North Chicago. The car was built at Highwood Shops in 1920. The derrick could be used as a posthole digger or as a pole setter; car is now at the Illinois Railway Museum.

———————————

Below left: Inactive for a number of years, plow #238 rusts and rots away on a siding at Pettibone Yard in January of 1963. Plow #238 was scrapped at Rondout in February of 1964.

———————————

Below right: Steeplecab #457 rusts away at Pettibone Yard in October of 1963. The North Shore ceased operations in January of 1963, so the future of this freight motor looks bleak. Steeplecab #457 was built in 1929 for the Arkansas Valley Interurban Railway. In 1942 the motor was purchased by the North Shore. Reversible trolley poles shown permit using both poles at the same time for increased power when hauling a heavy train.

Above left: Steeplecab #452 at Pettibone Yard in April of 1962 was built by General Electric in 1917 and handled North Shore freight efficiently through the years.

Above right: At Pettibone Yard, double-ended plow #605 sits on a siding during the summer months. Plow #605 was built in 1921 by the Russell Snow Plow Co.

At left: One of three vintage 1909 #200 series wood combines built by Jewitt Car Co. sits on the ground at Pettibone Yard in 1958. The car, used for storage, was in good shape and had a new roof coating applied.

The brakeman walks up to talk to the engineer of steeplecab #455, which is switching loads of ballast at North Chicago in 1961. Steeplecab #455, built in 1927 by GE, has been quite busy, spreading the fresh ballast on both main line tracks. In addition to trolley poles, #455 was equipped with batteries to service industries without trolley wires. *Collection of Arnie Burchardt*

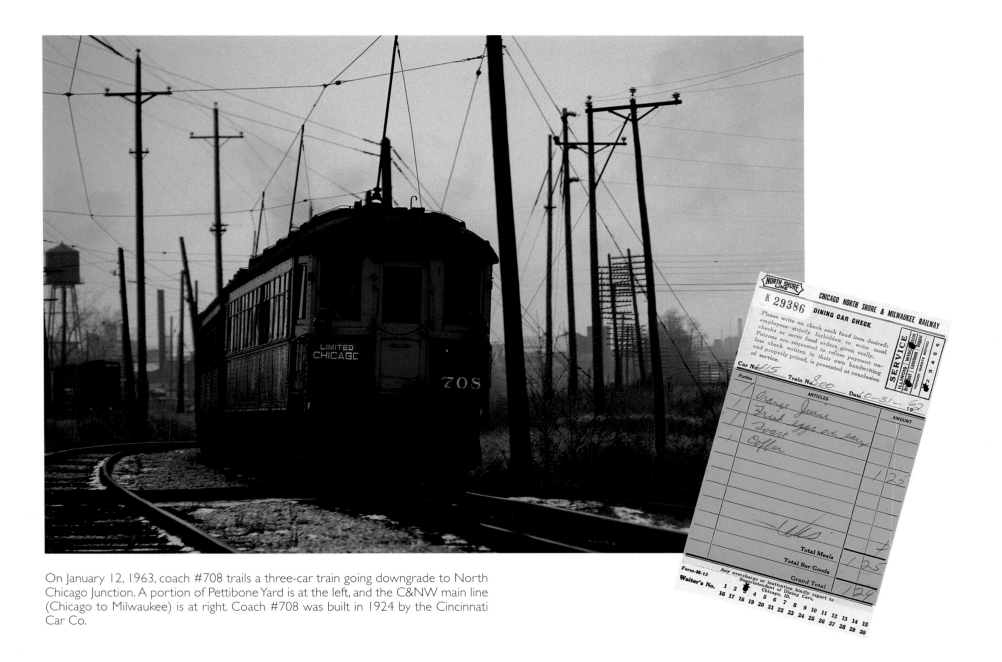

On January 12, 1963, coach #708 trails a three-car train going downgrade to North Chicago Junction. A portion of Pettibone Yard is at the left, and the C&NW main line (Chicago to Milwaukee) is at right. Coach #708 was built in 1924 by the Cincinnati Car Co.

Above: At Pettibone Yard in 1963, 100-ton articulated freight locomotive #459 shows off its articulation and unusual trolley pole arrangement. The double trolley poles were used to draw enough power to operate the eight traction motors. Locomotive #459 was built by the Oregon Electric Railway in 1941 and purchased by the North Shore in November of 1947. *Collection of Arnie Burchardt*

At left: In June, 1962, 100-ton articulated locomotive #458 basks in the sunshine outside the engine shed at Pettibone Yard. This locomotive was well suited for fast main line service. However, crews preferred sister locomotive #459, which had a center cab for better visibility during switching moves. Locomotive #458 was built by the Oregon Electric Railway in 1940 and purchased by the North Shore in December of 1947. *Collection of Arnie Burchardt*

At right: After alighting from a train, sailors stride toward the station at North Chicago Junction enroute to the Naval station at Great Lakes. On weekends, North Shore trains were filled with sailors eager to have fun in either Chicago or Milwaukee.

Below: This is a night-time view of the maintenance department at Highwood, Illinois in 1962. Electroliner #801-802, left, Silverliner #762 and an unknown sister fill up the space. Sets of trucks and parts are ready to be worked on. Silverliner #762 was built in 1930 by the Standard Steel Car Co. and rebuilt to a Silverliner in 1956.

Heavy repairs were made through the years at the Highwood Shops. It's hard to imagine, but work on rolling stock continued almost to the last day of railroad operation. The ghostly figure of a workman appears underneath coach #722, the result of a long exposure with a tripod-equipped cable release camera. Coach #722 was built by the Cincinnati Car Co. in 1926.

Above: Here's a glimpse to the past. This dispatcher tower was located at the west end of Highwood Shops trackage, which blended into the main line. Brakeman lanterns and a destination sign add much to an era that has vanished. *Collection of Russ Porter*

Above left: A trio of steeplecab freight motors, with only the front unit working, takes a freight east from Mundelein, Illinois in 1958. Steeplecab #454 was built by GE in 1923.

Below left: Coach #410 was built in 1923 by the Cincinnati Car Co. as a parlor car with an open observation platform. The Depression eliminated parlor car service, and #410 and three other parlor cars were stored until WWII. During that time they were converted into coaches and ended their days running between Chicago and Mundelein. Car #410 is shown at Mundelein in January of 1963; it was scrapped at Rondout in March of 1964.

The Mundelein station of 1926 was one of nine designed in the Spanish Colonial or Mission styles for the North Shore and South Shore lines by architect Arthur Gerber. Coach #177 stands next to the station, ready to depart for Chicago, in June of 1958. In back of #177, two Silverliners are on the storage tracks, while the one to the right is ready to move down to the station, once #177 departs.

Above: Coach #172 brings up the rear of the five-car train waiting for the later rush hour traffic to begin. For now, coach #177 is sufficient for mid-day eastbound traffic. Both coaches were built in 1920 by the Cincinnati Car Co.

At right: In April of 1964, a closeup shows the beautiful gold leaf lettering and details of the Mundelein station. Unfortunately, the Community Park District has put up its sign indicating ownership of the building. Today, no trace of the station or right-of-way is visible, and only apartment houses and streets occupy the area.

At right: For a few blocks west of the Mundelein station, there were several tracks for storing equipment between the morning and evening rush hours. Coach #715 is the end car of such stored equipment. Car #715 was built in 1926 by the Cincinnati Car Co.

———————————————

Below: Fantrip photographers have a field day at Mundelein station in March, 1962. A couple with their young children pose for a photograph alongside #251, the only combine modified as a Silverliner in 1953. Combine #251 eventually went to the Illinois Railway Museum.

Above: Coach #410 rests between other coaches on a storage track at Mundelein in 1961. The near end of #410 was formerly the open observation end.

At left: In 1958, coach #410, formerly an observation parlor car, enjoys the morning sun on a storage track at Mundelein.

Above: The line west from Lake Bluff ends here at the west end storage tracks at Mundelein. In May of 1961, six cars sit on the ready track, with coach #729 at the end of the line. The single track at extreme left is an interchange track with the Soo Line. Coach #729 was built in 1926 by the Cincinnati Car Co.

At right: Coming or going, the eastbound Electroliner at Briargate heading for Chicago, looks good at either end, thanks to a good design and attractive paint scheme.

Above: In January of 1963 a car from Mundelein is at Lake Bluff Junction. This is where the Skokie Valley Line branches west from the Milwaukee - Chicago main line and goes to Mundelein.

At left: One of only two built by GE in 1927, steeplecab freight motor #456 was equipped with overhead trolley wires or batteries. Thus, #456 could service industries without overhead electric wires. In 1960, #456 was northbound at Oakton curve. *Collection of Arnie Burchardt*

Above: Ballast train with steeplecab freight motor #455 works the main line, sandwiched between the fast passenger trains, at Lake Bluff, Illinois in 1961. *Collection of Arnie Burchardt*

At left: Line car #606 sits on a siding at Briargate in October of 1961. Car #606 was built in 1923 by the Cincinnati Car Co. and was retired to the railroad museum at Noblesville, Indiana. *Collection of Arnie Burchardt*

Bending around the curve at South Upton, Illinois, articulated freight motor #458 with 1,120 hp shows no effort as it moves a short train of ballast hoppers in October of 1961. *Collection of Arnie Burchardt*

At Evanston, Illinois in 1910, merchandise dispatch car #6 has just finished loading the horse-drawn wagon, and everyone relaxes to pose for the cameraman. *Collection of Russ Porter*

The C&NW suburban coach yard in Evanston appears on the left as Merchandise dispatch car #6 fills up three wagons on a somewhat bleak day in 1910. *Collection of Russ Porter*

Above: An Electroliner and combine #255 share tracks at the north end terminal of the North Shore at 12th St., Chicago, in June of 1962. The North Shore used the CTA's famous elevated loop to arrive here.

At left: An icy wind whirls around the stopped eastbound train at Dempster St. station, Skokie. It is the last day of full operation on the North Shore—January 20, 1963. The last coach #727 was chartered by the Wisconsin Chapter of the National Railway Historical Society for a trip over the entire line. Here, photographers on the left brave the wind and seven-below-zero temperatures to photograph the front side of the train. In the far distance is the tower at South Upton Junction where the North Shore crosses the C&NW freight line. Car #727 was built by the Cincinnati Car Co. in 1926.

At right: On January 20, 1963, from the vestibule of coach #727, a northbound train passes with coach #714 on the rear. A few passengers have just been picked up from the Great Lakes station. Coach #714 was built in 1926 by the Cincinnati Car Co. and eventually was retired to the Illinois Railway Museum.

Below: A desolate scene in February of 1963: looking north along the abandoned North Shore at Highwood is a long line of standard passenger cars. The upper floors of the general offices built in 1905 show above the roofs of the cars. To the right is one of the Electroliners and barely visible, some tracks away, is the other Electroliner.

This is a close look at Combine #255 at the 12th St. Terminal, Chicago, on January 20, 1963. Car #255 was built in 1917 by the Jewitt Car Co. Seats were removed in June of 1946 so space could be used for sailors' baggage going to and from the Great Lakes Naval Training Station.

Above: A Silverliner and standard coach are in the process of being cut up after torching at Rondout in December of 1963.

At left: In 1963-64, North Shore cars selected for scrapping were sent to Rondout where the North Shore interchanged with the Elgin, Joliet & Eastern. Cars were stored on the raised track which went west to Mundelein. When a car was ready for scrapping, a small diesel of the scrap firm pushed the car down to the ex-Elgin, Joliet & Eastern interchange track. There the car could be torched and cut up.

Below: This is a closeup of one of the torched standard North Shore coaches.

Above: In October of 1963, looking north on the abandoned North Shore right-of-way, it was hard to believe that 70 mph Electroliners passed over a crossing with the Chicago & North Western at this location known as "Ryan Tower." The tower on Ryan Rd. was west of Oak Creek, Wisconsin and was maintained by North Shore personnel.

At left: Its devilish work done, the scrap firm's diesel switcher is ready to leave the scrap track at Rondout in October of 1964. The abandoned embankment behind the switcher went east to Lake Bluff, Illinois.

At right: Wood snowplow meets a fiery end at Rondout in February of 1964. *Collection of Arnie Burchardt*

Below: Two North Shore coaches go up in flames at Rondout in January of 1964. *Collection of Arnie Burchardt*

Above: Looking northeast along the abandoned North Shore right-of-way in mid-1970, the Harrison Shop building appears at the extreme right. The tall smokestack at right belonged to the roundhouse of the abandoned C&NW Chase yards facilities in Milwaukee.

At right: A sign next to Ryan Road in 1966 shows the awaiting fate of the once-proud main line speedway of the North Shore Electroliners.

THIS PROPERTY
FOR SALE
FOR INFORMATION CONTACT
C. N. S. & M. RY.
REAL ESTATE DEPT. · HIGHLAND PARK, ILL.
IDLEWOOD 2-0500
WARNING

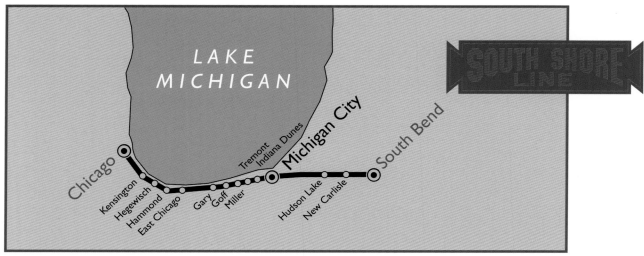

LAKE MICHIGAN

SOUTH SHORE LINE

Chicago
Kensington
Hegewisch
Hammond
East Chicago
Gary
Goff
Miller
Tremont
Indiana Dunes
Michigan City
Hudson Lake
New Carlisle
South Bend

CHICAGO SOUTH SHORE & SOUTH BEND RAILROAD

It's 2:38 p.m. according to the Coca-Cola sign and clock located on Chicago's famous Michigan Avenue in August of 1969. Almost in the shadow of the sign is the South Water Street stations of the Illinois Central and South Shore railroads. The IC tracks went underground to the terminal, and the South Shore tracks remained above ground. Midway between the morning and evening rush hours, it was a scene of tranquillity.

Above: Coach #12, Pullman-built in 1926, and its train, have just pulled into Randolph St. terminal on an October day in 1966, while on the next track, combine #100 and its train is ready to depart for South Bend, Indiana. Car #100 was also built in 1926 by Pullman. Tracks on the left descend into the IC's terminal at Randolph St.

At right: Coach #20 and baggage #504 are just about ready to depart from Chicago's Randolph St. terminal in March, 1964. Coach #20 was built by Pullman in 1927, lengthened in 1946, and retired in 1975. Baggage #504 was built by the St. Louis Car Co. in 1926 for the Indiana Railroad as car #377. South Shore rebuilt the car in 1955 with an additional baggage door, and removed the windows. Behind #504 looms a portion of the Prudential Insurance building.

A South Shore train with combine #109 leading passes the IC suburban coach yard at 18th St. in December of 1971. Car #109 was built in 1926 by Pullman, lengthened in 1944, and air conditioning and wide windows added in 1949. The car was retired in March of 1983 and was transferred to the Boone & Scenic Valley Railroad in Boone, Iowa. Notice how the colorful South Shore cars stand out against the somber dark color of the IC cars.

Bound for Gary, combine #108 passes the IC's suburban coach yard in October, 1971. Car #108 was built by Pullman in 1926, lengthened in 1943, with air conditioning and wide windows added in 1949. It was retired in 1977 and then went to the trolley museum at Noblesville, Indiana.

Above: A few moments more and the northbound train passes under the 18th St. bridge with combine #106 bringing up the rear. A few more gentle curves over the new ballast and the train will be at the terminal. Rush hour activity will soon bring alive the IC cars in the adjoining yard. Combine #106 was built by Pullman in 1926 and lengthened in 1943 with air conditioning and wide windows added in 1949.

At left: A northbound three-car train passes Roosevelt Rd. station in December, 1971 on its way to the end of South Shore tracks at Randolph St. In the upper left background the skeleton framework of McCormick Place convention center comes together.

At left: A close up view of new car #14 shows its pleasing appearance of still being an interurban car with the South Shore emblem and maroon and orange stripes through the middle of the windows. The doors at each vestibule end have steps for high and low platform loading. Automatic air and electrical connections in the couplers eliminates the need for jumper cables as used in the older cars.

Below: In November, 1988, #21 and its sisters sit at Randolph St. during a brief period of inactivity. The addition of new platforms and sheltering roofs gives an impression of a railroad making a good recovery from bad times.

Above: A winter storm is moving in fast from Lake Michigan and the temperature is below zero, so the rear red markers of car #19 are a welcome sight to the traveler about to enter the warm car. In a few minutes, train #603 will depart for Michigan City.

At left: With Michigan Avenue and its large skyscrapers in the background, the new South Shore cars with their platform roofs lend a pleasing perspective to this November, 1988 Chicago scene. At extreme right, an IC train heads south.

Below left: At Randolph St., Train #504 has just arrived from South Bend's Airport. Car #32 shows off its long length of 85 ft. and a pair of center doors without steps for loading at stations with high platforms. Single arm pantographs, instead of the diamond-shaped pantographs of the old cars, set off the modern appearance of each car.

Below right: When the new platforms and roofs were installed at Randolph St. in Chicago, another welcome sight was the lighted train sign. It shows Track Number, Departure Time and Stops along the way. No mistaking that Train #505 is to depart at 11:59 a.m., and the final stop is South Bend Airport.

Above: Locomotive #803, one of three 5,600 hp GE locomotives in main line freight service, switches cars on the IC and South Shore railroads interchange trackage at Kensington, Illinois. Fifteen of these locomotives were built in 1949 for shipment to Russia during the Joseph Stalin regime but never were shipped, thus the nickname "Little Joe." Russia could not pay for the locomotives, so the Milwaukee Road got 12 and the South Shore the remaining three.

At right: A 1973 Chicago-bound South Shore train waits for the IC suburban train to clear the junction at Kensington. There, the South Shore has trackage rights over IC tracks to Randolph St.

Once clearance is given, a three-car train, with car #38 trailing moves forward onto IC tracks. Coach #38 was built by the Standard Car Co. in 1929 and retired in December, 1982 and then was sent to the Boone & Scenic Valley Railroad.

Above: In May of 1968, the engineer awaits a backup signal from the brakeman at the Illinois-Indiana state line at Burnham Yard. Both #702 and #701, ex-NYC 3,000 hp locomotives purchased in October of 1955, were rebuilt between 1955 and 1958. Of the 10 purchased, only seven were rebuilt using parts of the other three. All seven locomotives were scrapped in 1976.

At left: A South Shore train passes Kensington tower which controls all train movements there. The tower handles a huge amount of IC suburban, main line passenger and freight, plus South Shore freight and passenger traffic.

At right: Freight motors #702 and #701 begin heading out of Burnham Yard toward Hammond and points east in May, 1968. These two units in outward appearance changed little from the NYC design with the unbroken roof line.

Below: It's hard to believe these units shown in May of 1968 in their bright traction orange colors were once black New York Central freight motors.

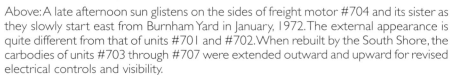

Above: A late afternoon sun glistens on the sides of freight motor #704 and its sister as they slowly start east from Burnham Yard in January, 1972. The external appearance is quite different from that of units #701 and #702. When rebuilt by the South Shore, the carbodies of units #703 through #707 were extended outward and upward for revised electrical controls and visibility.

At left: A freight train, led by motor #707, with black and white high visibility striping, is ready to move east from Burnham Yard in September of 1971. Behind the train appears the many yard tracks. Here, the South Shore interchanged with the Belt Railway of Chicago, the C&O and the Indiana Harbor Belt.

At right: Main line "Little Joe" freight motor #802 awaits assignment at Burnham Yard in November of 1965. Motor #802 was retired in 1981 and went to the Baltimore & Ohio Railroad Museum in Baltimore.

Below: Three freight units—#705, 706 and 707—bask in the cold afternoon sun at Burnham Yard in December, 1972. The #700 series of freight motors was well suited for short main line trains and could negotiate industrial sidings where the big Little Joes could not go.

At right: Freight unit #801 idles quietly in May of 1968 while awaiting cars to be delivered via Conrail to Burnham Yard. At left, a clutter of railroad tank car bodies await scrapping, a similar fate for #801 in 1981.

Below: Shiny Little Joe brings a train of freight cars out of Burnham Yard in January of 1973. In another minute, it will swing onto the main line and move eastward toward Michigan City.

With the street crossing sign flashing, a three-car train, headed for South Bend, starts slowing for a stop at the Hammond station in November, 1966. The last car, #203, is a trailer built in 1927 and lengthened in 1947.

In May of 1968 a two-car South Bend-bound train stops at the Hammond station to discharge and pick up passengers. This station is the first stop eastbound into Indiana and a major stop on the railroad. The unique station with the overhead electric sign and the baggage wagon all give the scene a distinctive interurban flavor. Rear car #26 was built in 1929 by the Standard Car Co., lengthened in 1948 and rebuilt with air conditioning and wide windows. In 1983 car #26 went to the South Shore Mall at Chesterton.

Above: A modernized combine and a standard coach pick up speed going past the Burnham Yard east entrance. The white cloud of smoke above the combine's roof is emitting from the steel mills at Hammond. On the left a battered gondola sits in front of one of the colorful homebuilt cabooses. The foreground track is C&O.

At left: Train #508 coming from the South Bend Airport gathers speed after leaving the Hammond station in November of 1995. After almost 13 years of service, the new cars have proven to be reliable for on-time performance and provide for low maintenance costs.

At right: On an overcast day in 1979, a Little Joe freight motor with caboose trailing slowly comes past the picturesque Hammond station. Loco #802 is heading east to the power plant at Michigan City to pick up a load of empty coal hoppers. Passengers on the platform wait for an eastbound train.

Below: A two-car train from South Bend accelerates rapidly after a short stop at the Hammond station in June, 1969. Differences in the window arrangement of each car are apparent: leading coach #15 has the original narrow windows, while the combine has the wide windows added in 1949. Coach #15 was built in 1926 and lengthened in 1942.

Passengers board a Chicago-bound train at Hammond in October of 1972. The conductor offers assistance and directions to one of the passengers, while another trainman talks to others. Car #36 was built by the Standard Car Co. in 1929.

Past the maze of tracks and switches at the east end of Burnham Yard, a two-car passenger train just minutes out of Hammond station heads for Chicago in May, 1968.

With its front end looking the worst for wear, combine #107 with a companion comes to a stop at the Hammond station. It's a cold day in November, 1966 and passengers stand patiently waiting to board while the conductor on the second car gets ready to help passengers off and on. Combine #107 was built by Pullman in 1926, lengthened in 1944, with air conditioning and wide windows added in 1949.

Above: Veteran coach #1 brings up the rear of a three-car train from South Bend, stopping briefly at Hammond in October of 1972. Coach #1 was the first car of an order of 15 steel coaches built by Pullman in 1926. The car had a smoking compartment, which was removed in 1964.

At left: A few blocks away from the Hammond station is this gem of a warning sign, photographed in November of 1966.

Huge GE Little Joe dwarfs the automobile and station at Hammond on a cold day in November of 1979. Surprising enough, there is no snow on the ground, as this area is known for early heavy snow.

A Chicago-bound two-car train slowly approaches the Hammond station in November of 1966. A number of passengers wait on the platform, while a city bus idles behind the crossing gate. Just above the bus is the familiar South Shore sign, a beautiful sight at night.

At left: Built by Pullman in 1927, coach #22 brings a train from South Bend into the Hammond station on a very warm day in June of 1975, as indicated by the attire of the crowd waiting to board. Coach #22 was lengthened in 1945 and received wide windows in 1960. Car #22 went to the Seaboard Railroad Museum in Jacksonville, Florida.

Below: Twenty years later, with the exception of the Hammond station, changes are evident. Catenary bridges over the tracks are gone, as is the old South Shore sign, which has been replaced with a more modern sign. Even the old orange cars are gone, but their replacements are a welcome sight in November of 1995.

Above: Watching the speedometer creep up in the rear car of Train #505 was quite an experience. Smooth operation over the well maintained track, plus superb truck suspension and quietness of the carbody structure, was a tribute to the Japanese and American companies responsible.

At right: In December, 1985, the view from the rear window vestibule of eastbound Train #505 traveling to South Bend, shows westbound Train #506 heading for Chicago. Just ahead of #506 is the curve leading to the bridge over the Norfolk & Western (ex-Nickel Plate Road) tracks.

Just west of Gary in December of 1973, combine #109 heads west through the unique gantlet bridge over the Pennsylvania and Norfolk & Western tracks. To save money, the South Shore engineering department initiated the idea of having eastbound and westbound tracks overlap each other on the bridge, thus eliminating switches at each end. Combine #109 was built in 1926 by Pullman and lengthened with wide windows in 1949.

The gantlet track design is clearly shown from the rear window vestibule of eastbound Train #505, headed for South Bend.

With the signal showing green, a westbound train from Gray picks up speed on the grade to the gantlet track bridge. Some switching of cars at South Bend station has been completed, as the rear car had been sitting idle long enough to have snow cover the roof. The first layer of snow on this October 18, 1972 has filtered down on the local landscape.

In June 1978, Little Joe #803, recently painted, brings a freight train of empty coal hoppers through a bridge near Gary. Locomotive #803 was built in 1949. The locomotive now resides at the Illinois Railroad Museum in Union, Illinois.

Looking the worse for wear, and downgraded to local freight switching, Little Joe #803 goes about its chores at Gary in January of 1981.

Going back in time to January, 1958, Little Joe #803 heads westward with a short freight train at Gary. The bright sunshine belies the fact that it is a very cold winter day.

Above: Nine-year-old Little Joe #803 leads its freight west at Gary in January of 1958. The big GE motor still has 23 more years of active service left before retiring to the Illinois Railroad Museum.

At left: The brakeman has just lined up the Pennsylvania interchange track at Gary in January of 1981 and is hurrying back to the warmth of a Little Joe's cab. A few minutes later #803 will start shoving the short string of cars down the incline.

An empty unit coal train, powered by Little Joe #803, rumbles west through the lush, green countryside near Gary in June, 1978. The GE motor has picked up its train at the power plant at Michigan City.

Above: With its headlight burning, coach #30 is ready to head west from the Gary station in December of 1970. It was built in 1929 by the Standard Steel Car Co., and when retired, it went to the East Troy Electric Railroad at East Troy, Wisconsin.

At right: Trailer #202 and combine #101 sit on the storage tracks at Gary during a January, 1971 mid-day lull. This entire area changed when the track was elevated in the mid-50s to run alongside the Indiana Tollway at left. The station was demolished and replaced by a modern facility. Trailer #202 was built in 1927 and lengthened in 1947. Combine #101, built by Pullman in 1926, went to the trolley museum at Noblesville.

Car #14 starts east across Broadway on its way to Michigan City in December of 1973. Hard to believe this Gary scene has entirely disappeared with the tracks elevated and the station replaced.

At right: EMD SW-1 switcher #601 sits in the shadow of trailer #212 in the yard at Gary in December, 1958. It was built in 1940 and had three previous owners: Buffalo Creek, Columbus & Greenville and Babcock & Wilcox. It came to the South Shore in October of 1956. Trailer #212 was built by the Standard Steel Car Co. in 1929 and scrapped in 1972.

Below: A late passenger hastens to the Gary station as westbound car #14 clears Broadway in December of 1973.

Next page: Photographers have a perfect setting, lighting and weather as westbound Train #508 picks up passengers at Dune Park, Indiana on a September day in 1992.

Above: In June 1968, westbound Little Joe #803 with an empty coal unit train from the Michigan City power plant, passes Beverly Shores. Now a private residence, the building nearest the track was the ticket office, while the building at the rear was the home of the ticket agent.

At left: Another view of massive Little Joe freight motor #803 as it is about to cross the road at Beverly Shores. With 5,600 hp, #803 has little trouble pulling the long line of coal empties across the almost-level Indiana countryside.

Above: In September of 1969, a portable sub-station is on a new siding near Gary. The years have been kind to this equipment; it has been given the utmost in care, as it has to be ready to move for any power emergency.

At right: GP-7 #5747 leading powers a freight through Gary during the last month in 1973. It was built by EMD in 1951 for the C&O. In 1971 the #5747 was leased to the South Shore, and later it was numbered #1503 for the South Shore and then returned to the C&O in 1981.

Combine #101, with red marker lights glowing, is part of a train wending its way down a Michigan City street in June, 1970. The warning sign at right has to be taken seriously as an accident from a power pole falling could result in a fire or explosion, or both.

Violent winter storms off the east shore of Lake Michigan can produce scenes as depicted in this oil painting of coach #9 at the Michigan City station. The big, heavy interurban cars will get through the storm unless city traffic snarls up, in spite of the approaching snow plow. Coach #9 was built by Pullman in 1926 and ended up at the East Troy, Wisconsin trolley museum.

Above: Eastbound Train #605 is just about to cross the N&W tracks at the entrance to Shops Yard at Michigan City in December, 1985. The curving track at the right interchanges with the N&W track at right.

At right: Looking the worse for wear, #1171 was used now and then in maintenance-of-way work. It sits on a rusty track at the Shops Yard in Michigan City in September of 1969.

At right: Little Joe freight motor #803 idles at Shops Yard, while the crew is in the office getting orders for the afternoon run to Burnham Yard. Date: June, 1978.

_____

Below: The fireman leans out of his window to talk to a photographer on the ground. The engineer of #803 is already giving the big unit a taste of power on this warm day in June of 1978.

Above: Little Joe #803 heads for the N&W crossing at Michigan City, and its final destination—Burnham Yard.

At right: On December 7, 1985, passenger train #608 stands ready to leave the Michigan City Shops Yard. Two EMD GP-38-2 diesel freight units with a caboose are heading for a service track. The two units were part of an order for 10 units received in January, 1981.

Above: On a cold February day in 1985, GP-38-2 diesel freight unit #2008 stands idle outside the shop building at Michigan City. Although ordered new from EMD, the 10 units were not painted in the South Shore's traction orange.

At left: South Shore's first freight diesel #601 sits near rival electric freight motor #703 at Shops Yard in September of 1961. Unit #703 was one of 10 acquired from the New York Central in 1954-55.

At left: GP-38-2 diesels #2006 and #2009 have just been serviced and are lined up on the ready track for assignment at Shops Yard in December of 1986.

Below: At Shops Yard in early 1958, freight motor #342 is the lead unit in a line of ex-NYC freight motors purchased by the South Shore in 1954-55. In June of 1958, #342 came out of the Shops Yard paint department with bright traction orange paint and a new number—706.

The diesel's orange is quite a contrast from the somber black of ex-NYC #342.
Locomotive #704 switches an empty box car at Shops Yard in September of 1961.

Shops Yard storage tracks in September of 1961 have an assortment of equipment: box cars in the foreground, Little Joe #801, the only #800 series to be scrapped in 1981 (the other two went to museums), a number of cabooses, two #1000 series locomotives, another Little Joe hiding behind a pole, one #700 series locomotive and the #601 diesel switcher.

Above: A Little Joe and combine #108 face each other on a yard track at Shops Yard in 1964. Combine #108 was built by Pullman in 1926, lengthened in 1943, with wide windows added in 1949. Some prankster has tacked a U.S. highway sign below the stop sign, while the sign on the right indicates that it is a private road.

At right: Glistening in new paint, lengthened coach #27 stops for a few minutes while a workman checks the step mechanism. Car #27 was built by the Standard Car Co. in 1929, and scrapped at the Shops Yard. Assorted freight motors on the yard tracks at right await assignments in December of 1973.

All three Little Joes appear to have been recently painted on this day in December, 1973. Locomotive #803 seems to have had the most freight service of the three motors, as it appears in most of the photographs along the main line.

At right: Freight motors #902 and #900, ex-Illinois Central Baldwins built in 1929, rest on storage tracks alongside ex-NYC freight motors at Shops Yard on September, 1961.

Below: Little Joe #802, a trifle grimy, awaits maintenance work on its wheels in March, 1978.

Viewed from the highway bridge overlooking Shops Yard in December of 1973, the nicely-painted Little Joes make an impressive sight towering over other equipment in the yard.

Above: Lengthened and with wide windows, combines #104 and #106 show off recently-painted exteriors in the warmth of a building at Shops Yard in 1973.

At right: In December of 1974 a view into the underbody and pantograph repair building at Shops Yard shows coach #33, combine #110 and line car #1100. Coach #33 was built by the Standard Car Co. in 1929. Combine #110 was built by the Standard Car Co. in 1929 as coach #10 and rebuilt as combine #119 with air conditioning and wide windows. It was scrapped at Shops Yard. Line car #1100 was built by the St. Louis Car Co. in 1926 for the Indiana Railroad as combine #376, and rebuilt as a line car in 1947 by the South Shore.

Above: A day in March, 1964 finds the maintenance department at Shops Yard filled with equipment. Coach #17 has had its roof painted and soon will have the railway name applied to the letterboard above the windows. It was built by Pullman in 1927. Short coach #8 is awaiting rebuilt pantographs and trucks. It was built by Pullman in 1926 and went to the Illinois Railroad Museum in 1982.

At right: A photographer admires the classic style of line car #1100 sheltered inside at Shops Yard in December, 1975.

In August of 1974, coach #8 still remains in the maintenance department, but on a different track; diesel switcher #601 is in for truck and engine repairs. Coach #38 is in for wheel replacement, and combine 108 at left is having roof work.

Above: Awaiting word for possible overhead wire repair, line car #1100 shows off its true interurban design, despite the cluttered roof. The girder type platform on the roof can swing out over two other tracks for servicing the wires. It sits on a siding with a trolley wire coil gondola at Shops Yard in 1961.

At left: In 1973 outside the Shops Yard buildings, line car #1100 still looks good. An effort to partially repaint the car is apparent with the deeper shade of orange on the front window frames and side doors. Car #1100 has the distinction of being the oldest operating interurban car in regular use. This photo was taken at Shops Yard in December of 1973.

Line car #1100 passes two of the #700 freight motors as it comes off the main line into the yard tracks at Shops. Most wire problems occur during the winter months, so #1100 is kept busy.

Above: A contrast in colors is evident in viewing these cabooses at the Michigan City yards in March of 1964. Freshly painted #1067 was built by the South Shore at the Michigan City Shops in the early 1950s. Caboose #1059 was also built there around 1946.

At right: In 1978, ex-C&O caboose still carries a C&O number as it basks in the sunlight outside a shop building at Michigan City.

A brand new South Shore hopper car shows off its red paint job on a storage track at Shops Yard in December, 1985.

Car #503 was originally built by the St. Louis Car Co. in 1926 as mail car #375 for the Indiana Railroad. It was rebuilt by the South Shore in 1952 with an extra baggage door added and windows removed. It was used as a storage car at Shops Yard in December of 1985.

Left: Train #3605 from Chicago heads for the yard after discharging its last passengers at the Carrol Avenue, Shops Station in Michigan City. The late afternoon sun casts long shadows on this very cold day in December of 1985.

Below: Little Joe #803 brings a local freight train west from Michigan City in June, 1978. Sometime later #803 or a sister freight motor will move the empty unit coal hoppers on the adjacent track from the nearby power plant.

Above: The interior of one of the new Japanese-American cars has a pleasant appearance. The middle doors next to a large washroom separate two seating sections. One half has the seats facing forward, and the other half has the seats facing backward, thus eliminating the need to turn seats around. Riding qualities of the new cars are comparable to those of Amtrak equipment.

Above: Locomotive #803 rumbles around an industrial spur to deliver a box car to an on-line customer at Michigan City in June, 1978.

At right: Combine #101 makes its way through downtown traffic in South Bend in June, 1970. #101's destination is the big red building at the left, just a few blocks away.

The cooling tower of the Michigan City power plant looms in the distance as #803 comes to a halt and head brakeman and engineer decide how the cars will be switched. Behind the gate marked with a red "x" are the storage tracks for the power plant unit coal train hoppers.

In June of 1970 the engineer looks back as the conductor helps passengers alight onto the dirt road from combine #101 at the west end of South Bend. The crossing in front of #101 is an unused spur of the New York Central.

Coach #24 leads a two-car train eastbound in the west end of South Bend in June, 1970. Coach #24 was built by Pullman in 1927, and lengthened and rebuilt with air conditioning and wide windows in 1947. It eventually went to the trolley museum at East Troy.

Coach #11 brings up the rear of an eastbound train going down La Salle St. in South Bend. A youngster in non-air conditioned #11 is fascinated by the steam vapor arising from the traction motors, as the cars wade through a puddle of water in June, 1970. Coach #11 was built in 1926 by the Pullman Co. and lengthened in 1945.

In May 1969, combines #100 and #108 line up side by side in the small coach yard off La Salle St. in South Bend. A workman is inspecting the underbody of the car behind #108.

Above: Combine #104, headlight glowing, moves out of the South Bend coach yard on a June day in 1970. It will pick up its first passengers at the downtown La Salle St. station, just a few blocks away. This yard and the La Salle St. station disappeared from the scene when a new line was built to the South Bend airport.

At left: After leaving the yard in June of 1970, combine #104 travels on La Salle St. toward the passenger station, whose sign shows through a portion of the pantograph on the right side of the roof. Since then, the station has been torn down and all tracks have been removed.

Above: The South Shore wanted to abandon street running because of automobile and truck traffic, which was a mess during rush hour and during the winter months. Combine #103 was built in 1926 and scrapped at Shops Yard.

At right: As Combine #108 comes to a stop at the downtown South Bend station in June of 1970, a swarm of passengers spill out onto La Salle St. It seems an impossible task to fit them all into the single car, but the conductor works a miracle.

Combine #103 pulls away from the South Bend station in June, 1970. The crowd at the station hasn't been left behind—it's waiting for the arrival of an eastbound train.

Above: With a crew exchange and passengers loaded, the forward pantograph ready to come down and the rear one ready to go up, combine #100 is ready to leave South Bend for Chicago in May of 1969.

At left: Combine #104 travels slowly along La Salle St. in South Bend, a street beset with automobile and truck congestion, traffic lights and deteriorating track in 1970.

Above: On January 6, 1996, Train #510 is ready to depart from the South Bend Airport over a new six-mile spur. The South Shore runs partially in South Bend, but oddly makes no stops for passengers to and from the airport. The first stop (a flag stop by day, a light by night) is at Hudson Lake, Indiana.

At right: A bumper post view of car #25 shows Train #510 about ready to leave the new South Bend Airport Station on January 6, 1996. The ultra-modern building, while looking nice, offers no protection for passengers against the winter wind and snow.

Index

North Shore Electroliner stops at 6th Street viaduct, Milwaukee, on a cold winter night as passengers stay warm inside the cars.